CRASH COURSE

on

Revelation

ΑΤΙΟΥΑΥΤΟΥΚΑΙΟ ΟΥΤΟ
ΟΙΗΨΑΝΤΟΔΙΕΣΩ ΤΟΣΤΟ
ΑΝ ΤΟΤΕΠΡΟΣΕΡΧ ΑΝΘΩ
ΛΙΤΩΙΥΑΠΟΙΕΡΟCOΛ ΠΟ
ΩΝΦΑΡΕΙCΑΙΟΙΚΑ
ΓΑΜΜΑΤΕΙCΛΕΓΟΝΤ
ΙΑΤΙΟΙΜΑΘΗΤ
ΑΡΑΒΑΙΝΟΥCΙΝ
ΑΡΑΔΟCΙΝΤ
ΥΠΕΡΦΑΛΟΥC
ΤΑCΧΕΙ
ΟΗΕCΟ
ΟΚΡΙC
ΑΤΙΚ
ΙΝΟΤ
ΥΤΟ
ΟΙΗ

CRASH COURSE
on
Revelation

SIX SESSIONS

CHRISTIANITY TODAY

INTERNATIONAL

BIBLE STUDY

Standard®
PUBLISHING
Bringing The Word to Life

www.standardpub.com

Published by Standard Publishing, Cincinnati, Ohio

www.standardpub.com

Copyright © 2009 by Christianity Today International

Editor: Brad Lewis

Creative Development Editors: Kelli B. Trujillo and Roxanne Wieman

Contributing Authors: Wayne Brouwer, Tom Cowan, Joy-Elizabeth Lawrence,
Brandon O'Brien, Timothy Peck, and JoHannah Reardon

Consultant: Dr. Robert Lowery, Professor of New Testament and Dean of Lincoln
Christian Seminary, Lincoln, Illinois

Cover and interior design: The DesignWorks Group

ISBN 978-0-7847-2250-3

15 14 13 12 11 10 09   9 8 7 6 5 4 3 2 1

CONTENTS

How to Use This Study in Your Group

As Christians, we are a people of the Book. We base most of our knowledge of God and our faith in God on what we read in the Bible. It's critically important that we continually take up our Bibles and pursue a greater understanding of the text and the God who is revealed through it. The goal of the Crash Course Bible Studies series is to help you and your group become more comfortable, knowledgeable, and interested in the Bible—to aid you in that great pursuit of discovering God through his written revelation.

So whether you're a brand-new Christian or a seasoned believer, whether you've read from the Bible every day of your life or are just cracking it open for the first time, you'll find in Crash Course new insights, fresh challenges, and material to facilitate dialogue.

REVELATION

Some Christians—even some well-educated Bible scholars—consider Revelation to be one of the most controversial and difficult books of the Bible, with many diverse interpretations of the meanings of the various names and events in the account. However, at the most basic level, Revelation is a book of hope. Its central message is that God and good will win over evil, no matter how bad things look now. In this study, you'll explore the basic themes of Revelation, its images and symbols, and various views on Christ's second coming and eternal rule. You'll also look at the Old Testament references John used in the book and the relevance of Revelation's message for today.

ABOUT THE SESSIONS

Each session in this book is designed for group use—either in a small group setting or adult Sunday school class. The sessions contain enough material to keep your group busy for a full ninety-minute small group time but can also be easily adapted to work in a shorter meeting time—a true crash course. Or if you'd like to spend even more time, feel free to take two weeks for each of the six sessions; that essentially provides a quarter of a year's worth of content for your group.

The readings, activities, and discussion questions will help your group dig deeper into the Bible passages, engage in thought-provoking dialogue, explore ways to personally apply the material . . . and get to know one another better! Every group member should have a copy of *Crash Course on Revelation,* both for at-home readings and for use during group time. As you go through the study during your group time, take turns reading aloud the text and questions in the book. That gives everyone a sense of participating in the study together.

Here's how each session breaks down:

Launch

At the beginning of each session, you'll find a great introduction to the topic (be sure to read this aloud at the beginning of your meeting!), a list of Scriptures you'll study during the session, any extra supplies to bring, and notes on anything else to prepare before the session.

There's also a launching activity to start your group time. This activity sets the stage for the week's topic and gets people ready to start talking!

Explore

Next up is the meat of the study—the "Explore" section. This portion includes several teaching points that each focus on a specific aspect of the broader session topic. As you explore each teaching point, you'll study some Scripture passages, interact with one another as you talk through challenging questions, and read commentary on the passages. Also included are excerpts from related Christianity Today International articles (more about that below) that will enrich group discussion. If you are leading the group, be sure to ask God to help you make his Word come alive for your group during this time of exploring his truth (see Hebrews 4:12).

Apply

The Christian life—the abundant life—is about more than just thoughtful study and dialogue. James says, "As the body without the spirit is dead, so faith without deeds is dead" (James 2:26). The "Apply" section of each session will help take your discussion and study to another level; it will help you *live out* the ideas and values from that session. During this time, each participant will choose from three different challenge options (or come up with their own) to do during the coming week. These challenges will help group members make what they've learned a part of their lives in a practical way.

Pray

Before you finish up, be sure to take some time to pray for one another. In the "Pray" section, you'll find an idea you can use for your group's closing prayer.

Before Next Time

Take a look at the "Before Next Time" box for a heads-up on what to read or prepare for your next meeting.

FOR FURTHER RESEARCH

Resource List

Located at the end of session 6 is a list of recommended resources that can help take your study on the topic even further. You'll want to check those out!

Christianity Today International Articles

You'll also find three bonus articles from Christianity Today International publications. These articles are written by men who have studied Revelation. The sessions reference the articles during the course of the study. These articles are meant to help your group dive deeply into the topic and discuss a variety of facts, thoughts, and opinions. Taking the time to read these articles (as well as anything else suggested in the "Before Next Time" box at the end of each session) will greatly enrich your group's discussion and help you engage further with each topic.

It's our prayer that *Crash Course on Revelation* will change the lives of your group members as you seek to better understand the basic themes and symbols of Revelation, how this book connects with the Old Testament, thoughts on the millennium as revealed in Revelation, and why the book is important for us today. May the Holy Spirit move in and through your group as you grow in your relationship with Christ and your knowledge of God's Word.

Basics | 1

Understanding the vision and promise God delivers
is crucial to understanding Revelation.

The first word of the book of Revelation is the Greek word that we translate as apocalypse.

We sometimes use the word apocalypse *to describe a tragedy or catastrophe. But the word literally means "to uncover," or "an unveiling." Something that has been hidden for some time is now being revealed. Before the days of digital photography, maybe you were in a darkroom and watched a photograph develop. Before your eyes, the image changed from being invisible to being visible. That's what John means at the beginning of this book.*

What does Revelation unveil? Essentially, John's revelation is an uncovering of Jesus Christ. It reveals who he is right now in power and glory, even though we can't see him.

ΙΗΤΑΝΤΟΔΙΕϹШΟΝΠΟΓΕΥΟΜΕΝΟ

Revelation was given to John so that the church could be prepared for Christ's final coming. The Christian life is to be lived in the light of the tension between what we already are in Christ and what we hope someday to be. Christ has already won the decisive battle (Revelation 1:5, 6; 5:5, 6), and we may look forward with great expectation to the day when God will bring to completion the work he has begun in us.

BIBLE BASIS: *Revelation 1:1-11, 12-20; Revelation 2–5*

EXTRA SUPPLIES: *recent copies of news magazines, such as* Time, Newsweek, *and* U.S. News & World Report; *a whiteboard (or a pad of blank newsprint) and markers*

BEFOREHAND: *Since this is the first week of your study, the leader should send out an e-mail to everyone in the group. Remind participants to purchase a copy of* Crash Course on Revelation *if they haven't already. Encourage group members to read the article "When You Feel You're at the End" by Jack Hayford (p. 67) in preparation for this week's session. Be sure to mention where and when you're meeting.*

LAUNCH

Pass around copies of the news magazines the leader brought. Break into groups of three or four people and do a little analysis by discussing the following questions:

- What kinds of stories do these publications feature on their covers?
- What do you notice about the blurbs on the cover? What style are they written in? What key words are meant to draw in readers?

Although you're just beginning your study, based on what you know, write a news magazine cover blurb for the book of Revelation in your smaller group. Come back together as a larger group and share your headlines or blurbs. The leader can write these on a whiteboard or newsprint so that everyone can see them.

 # EXPLORE

Teaching Point One: God gave the apostle John a vision not only for his benefit but also for ours.
Read Revelation 1:1-11.

John, the apostle who also wrote the Gospel of John, wrote Revelation. This took place on the island of Patmos (v. 9). This small island is about ten miles long and six miles wide, covered with rocks and sustained by little vegetation. The Alcatraz of the first century, it was obvious why the Romans used it as a penal colony and a place of exile: there was no escape from it. Hippolytus, one of the early church leaders, tells of John's suffering under the emperor Domitian. Hippolytus says that John was first plunged into boiling oil and then sent into exile.

Read the section titled "We Can Never Be in a Place Where Christ's Love Won't Find Us" in "When You Feel You're at the End" by Jack Hayford (p. 70).

Why do you think John was in exile in such an isolated place?

Where is your "Patmos"? In what areas of life do you feel the most desolate and obscure?

ІΗ✝ΑΝΤΟΔΙΕϹѠ⁰⁺ΠΟΓΕΥΟΜΕΝΟΓ

How does knowing that Jesus appeared to John in such a wretched place encourage you?

Read Revelation 1:12-20.

Verses 12-18 provide a picture of the exalted Christ that was given to John. The placing of this vision right at the beginning of the book is significant. The revelation is essentially the unveiling of who Jesus Christ is in power and in glory. It is a vision of who Jesus Christ is now, not who he will be. Read John 17:5, in which Jesus prayed to be returned to the glory he had before the world began.

The Message renders Revelation 1:12-18 like this:

I turned and saw the voice.

I saw a gold menorah with seven branches,

And in the center, the Son of Man, in a robe and gold breastplate, hair a blizzard of white,

Eyes pouring fire-blaze, both feet furnace-fired bronze,

His voice a cataract, right hand holding the Seven Stars,

His mouth a sharp-biting sword, his face a perigee sun.

I saw this and fainted dead at his feet. His right hand pulled me upright, his voice reassured me:

"Don't fear: I am First, I am Last, I'm Alive. I died, but I came to life, and my life is now forever. See these keys in my hand? They open and lock Death's doors, they open and lock Hell's gates."

Why do you think God gave this vision to John? How did John respond to the vision? What happened to him?

John called some of the symbols a "mystery" (v. 20). What do you think this says about how we should interpret Revelation?

How have you felt about the book of Revelation in the past? What in this first chapter of Revelation disturbs you? What excites you?

Teaching Point Two: It's helpful to observe the images of Revelation with a big-picture view.
Read Revelation 4 and 5.

The language and images throughout Revelation were well known and understood by its first-century readers. But that's definitely not the case for us. We have to work hard to grasp the meaning of its powerful symbolism, and we may not always succeed. Yet as we read its sweeping illustrations, we must also avoid the danger of "standing too close" to the passage. In other words, we must avoid the temptation to isolate truths from the framework of the book. If we try too hard to explain every detail, we may find ourselves unweaving the rainbow. When you do that, you no longer have a rainbow.

The book of Revelation is really a giant painting. Stand too close and you can't see it; it appears to be little more than a collection of brush strokes. So we have to stand back far enough to see the entire picture. That picture is Jesus.

Have you ever read through the entire book of Revelation? If so, what did you get out of it?

What are some ways that we can skew the meaning of the book of Revelation? How can we avoid doing this?

Why do you think God gave us some portions of Scripture, like Revelation, in apocalyptic language? Why did John use this style in Revelation?

Teaching Point Three: The seven churches have many life lessons for us. Read Revelation 2 and 3.

This book contains seven letters addressed to churches in the Roman province of Asia (present-day Turkey) to warn them against falling away from their faith in Christ. It also offered assurance of ultimate victory for those who remain on God's side.

Some Bible scholars believe that these letters simply provided a literary device that creates a framework for the book. However, it seems that the detail and the historical data are too accurate for this. We do know that these cities existed in the ancient world.

The structure of each letter includes a condemnation, a commendation, and a promise that the church will be victorious.

Here's a quick summary of the topic each of these seven letters addressed:

- Ephesus (2:1-7): the church that forgot its first love (v. 4)
- Smyrna (2:8-11): the church that suffered persecution (v. 10)
- Pergamum (2:12-17): the church that needed to repent (v. 16)
- Thyatira (2:18-29): the church with a false prophetess (v. 20)
- Sardis (3:1-6): the church that fell asleep (v. 2)
- Philadelphia (3:7-13): the church that endured patiently (v. 10)
- Laodicea (3:14-22): the church with lukewarm faith (v. 16)

Revelation 2:9, 10 provides a good example of what Jesus communicated to each church. What condemnation, commendation, and promise do you find in these verses?

Concerning their relationship with God, many Christians are like one or more of these churches. Which church are you most like? Why?

Like much of Revelation, the promises to these churches were written in symbolic language. What are some possible meanings for each of the seven promises?

APPLY

If the book of Revelation is just the hallucination of an old man in prison, we really have no hope. We're destined to live each day in the prison of life. We're prisoners of the cruelest of things—hopelessness.

But if John's vision is real, then the eyes of the Lord that looked down from the cross also look down from the place of glory where he now sits. The most transforming thing we can ever know is that we live each day in the light of the love of the Son of glory, who sits at the right hand of the Father in Heaven.

Perhaps you feel imprisoned on some "Patmos" in your own life—isolated and abandoned. Jesus looks down on you from glory. He can transform your "exile" into a place of ministry and service, flooding your life with hope.

Choose one of the following application options to do on your own this week. Turn to a partner and share your choice.

NEW IMAGE

The way John described Jesus in Revelation 1 is a long way from the paintings of the long-haired Jesus with the neatly trimmed beard that many of us grew up with. Spend some time writing in a journal or doodling on a sketch pad. With either words or drawings, describe what Jesus looks like to you. Think of how he appeared during his ministry on earth, and think of how he appears in Heaven now.

MORE WORD PICTURES

While the visions, images, and figurative language of Revelation can seem foreign to us, we actually use our own set of word pictures in our everyday lives. Remember metaphors and similes from freshman English class? This week, keep a list of the figurative language you often use (strong as an ox, quiet as a mouse . . .).

Ask God to use your list to help open your mind as you seek a better understanding of the images and language of Revelation.

WRITE A LETTER

What kind of letter would Jesus write to you, your small group, or your church? Try to write that letter yourself, considering what Jesus would criticize you for, what he would praise, and what promise of reward he would deliver.

 # PRAY

Each member should turn again to the seven churches' condemnations in Revelation 2, 3. Take a moment to skim the passage and silently choose which most closely represents an area where you're failing. Also look at the way the Lord commended that church, as well as the promise he gave. Then as a group, spend time in silent prayer, asking God to help each member recall his or her pertinent promise throughout the coming week.

BEFORE NEXT TIME: *The leader should secure artistic representations of Jesus based on the scenes of Revelation 1 (risen and glorious Christ), Revelation 5 (the Lion/Lamb), and/or Revelation 19 (great king on a horse at the head of heavenly armies). Look for these depictions online or in oversize books at the public library. Also needed is a map of the Aegean Sea showing the location of Patmos Island in relation to Turkey (Asia Minor) and Ephesus. The leader (or someone the leader assigns) can check the maps section of a study Bible for this. Everyone should read "The Gift of Vision" by Darrell Johnson (p. 77).*

Themes | 2

While the specific scenes of Revelation can be confusing,
key themes shine with great brilliance.

The bookends of the Bible seem to cause the most controversy. Few people argue over the value of the Old Testament's moral teachings or the urgency of its prophetic messages. Most also agree that Jesus' teachings are profound and relevant, and that the letters of the New Testament contain some of the most inspiring exhortations ever written.

But Genesis and Revelation confound us. After all, no one witnessed the origins of the universe. And Revelation—with its alarms of impending judgment and descriptions of Christ's glorious eternal rule—draws out many speculations and wildly diverging interpretations.

However, when we step back from the intensity of John's visions and take a fresh look at the big picture he sees, a number of clear themes emerge. We might argue over the meaning of the color of a

ΟΥΚΛΙΕΣΕΛΘΩΝΕΚΕΙΟCΝοΦΛΟΝΕ

horse or the time table of Revelation, but we can't miss the power released each time we see a vision of Jesus in these pages, the stifling pain of a world in crisis, or the great beauty and comfort of the final victory promised after the strife.

BIBLE BASIS: *Revelation 1–5; 12; 19:1-16; 21:1-7; 22:1-6*

EXTRA SUPPLIES: *artistic representations of Jesus, a map showing Patmos Island*

 LAUNCH

As the group comes together, spend some time looking at the pictures of Jesus provided by the leader. Talk with each other about your impressions, reactions, and feelings as you view each of these scenes. Then discuss the following questions:

- If you didn't know the titles of these portrayals and had to title them yourself, what would you name each one? Why?
- How do the pictures compare with your own mental image of Jesus?

 EXPLORE

Teaching Point One: It's all about Jesus.
Read Revelation 1.

Imagine John's experience. Near the end of the first century, he was the last of Jesus' disciples to remain alive. He had been shepherd of the great congregation in Ephesus for several decades. The Roman emperor Domitian came to power in AD 81 and was not favorable to the growing influence of Christianity. Some historians say Domitian was responsible for an empire-wide persecution of the followers of this new religion. After failing to kill John outright, Domitian sentenced him to exile at the penal colony on Patmos. There, during John's personal devotions on a Sunday morning, Jesus appeared to John in full glory.

Now notice the paradoxes. Domitian seemed to control all things, yet Jesus came as the supreme ruler of the universe. John had received a death sentence, yet was greeted as a victor by the one who conquered death itself.

Look at the map that was brought in, showing the isle of Patmos. When have you felt as though you'd received a death sentence? Or when have you simply felt spiritually isolated? How did Jesus meet you there?

Read Revelation 4 and 5.

Although he was isolated from the church and lacked the usual worship helps, John got caught up in the grandest scene of glory imaginable. Look at the descriptions John gave us: The great throne is at the center of all things. Because God can't be seen, John described him by way of reflections and shimmerings. John heard of Jesus' great power as symbolized by the Lion, but saw him as the sacrificial Lamb. The great chorus that reverberates throughout Heaven and earth and beyond is the song about Jesus the Savior.

What do you think this scene tells us about God?

What do you think this scene says about Jesus? (Try to base your answers directly on the words and images in Revelation 4, 5. For an extended treatment of this passage, read the section "God Is in Control and His Plan Is Secure" in "The Gift of Vision" by Darrell Johnson [p. 78].)

What do these descriptions tell you about the character and nature of God as he relates to you personally? How does God's power make you feel—like an aimless speck in the universe, an important part of God's plan, or something else? Explain.

Read Revelation 19:1-16.

Notice the movement of the book of Revelation when viewed around John's three great visions of Jesus. First, Jesus came to John as the powerful resurrected Lord. Then Jesus is the redeemer who paid the ultimate sacrifice for sin and gained authority to press divine terms against the nations of the earth. Finally, here, Jesus is the conquering king who finishes what he started and claims his own in a restoration of kingdom righteousness and peace.

While we might dispute the meaning of scenes and images in Revelation, we can't miss the reality that, first and foremost, this book is about Jesus. Jesus takes charge of a compromised and combative world. Jesus rules!

Why do you think this message of Jesus' rule was sent to the seven churches in chapters 2, 3? How might this message have affected them?

How does this message speak into your life today?

Teaching Point Two: The world is in crisis.
Read Revelation 2 and 3.

Jesus gave this revelation to John because specific congregations were struggling to stay faithful in a chaotic world. Some were persecuted and scorned for their beliefs. Others were compromising their faith—some perhaps afraid not to go along with the crowd, others deliberately blending false teachings with Christianity. But all of them were caught up in a war of values that demanded response. Coasting wasn't an option. Either Jesus was Lord over their lives, or they were giving allegiance to other loyalties. Trying to serve two masters was making life exacting and exhausting.

What kinds of religious and moral choices were these churches facing?

How do the pressures of these kinds of choices bear down on your daily life? What compromises tempt you on a daily basis? Why? What have you done in response?

Read Revelation 12.

Theologians take several different approaches to the book of Revelation.

The *preterist* view understands Revelation as a coded word of encouragement mostly intended for John's first-century community, with its symbols largely lost to us.

The *historicist* perspective finds the whole history of the church between Jesus' first and second comings outlined in these pages. So if we're wise and careful enough, we can find our specific location in time and interpret cryptic pictures that remind us of the battles we are currently facing.

The *idealist* view sees the book as a kind of allegory, with images and symbols that speak to us of the ongoing war between good and evil, between God and Satan, and between the church and the world. This view suggests that we shouldn't try to read too much into the specifics of each page, but rather catch the loud voice of Jesus that commands us to faithfulness through the trials of the hour.

Finally, a *futurist* perspective—popularized recently in novels and films— sees the action in Revelation as a looming and traumatic time just ahead.

Though interpretations are argued, a core theme is always clear: this world is in crisis, and the ways and the people of God are constantly under attack.

Why do you think a message of attack and warfare is necessary for the church (then and now) to hear? In general, how has the church responded to persecution since the time Revelation was written? How might Revelation have influenced that response?

Though persecution of Christians happens around the world today, we don't always experience overtly violent or oppressive persecution. Yet we're still under attack. What things subtly attack your faith on a daily basis? How do you survive and thrive during those times of attack?

Teaching Point Three: Living happily ever after isn't a fairy tale.
Read Revelation 21:1-7.

Few scenes in Scripture are as beautiful or powerful as this one. Notice that "a new heaven and a new earth" are remade by the cleansing power of God, and that those who rise again live on this new earth. Also notice how Heaven and earth are united in a way that allows God, angels, and humans all to see one another directly, without the sharp distinctions between the spiritual and material worlds that mark our current age.

The church in John's day experienced heated persecution. Many Christians had lost their lives, and those who remained on earth were largely the underclasses of society. How would this part of Revelation have spoken to John's initial readers? What assurances could they "take home" after hearing these words?

What do you think the world will be like after Jesus returns? What Scriptures give you that idea?

What message from this passage resonates with you for today?

Read Revelation 22:1-6.

The images in this passage come directly from the prophecies of Ezekiel. Ezekiel wanted the people of Judah, languishing in Babylonian exile around 550 BC, to get homesick for Palestine once again and to hunger for God's restoration that would heal their nation. John used the same scenes to call his readers to a deep thirst for global renewal—a time when wars will end, diseases will vanish, crops will thrive, laughter will be the primary language of children, and hope will be the confident stature of the nations.

How often do you pray for Jesus' return and the renewal of this world? Why? What are you hoping for?

 APPLY

The book of Revelation starts off with a bang (Jesus' sudden and overwhelming appearance to John), marches along to drumbeats and war trumpets, and then finishes with the lyrical sentimentality of a great love story. However, throughout the book—amid the flurry of images and cryptic descriptions— rings the constant theme that Jesus is in charge. He is before all things, over all things, in all things, through all things, and the destiny of all things. This comfort sustains us when we go through our own mysterious times, when things don't make sense, and when life turns against us in a hundred different ways.

When challenges come—and they will—remember these themes and catch John's vision of a world waiting to be reborn.

Choose one of the following application options to do on your own this week. Turn to a partner and share your choice.

RECOVER PERSPECTIVE

Take the latest issues of a newspaper or a news magazine and write across each page in large letters with a black marker: "King Jesus is in charge." Think about what this means in relation to the primary story on one or more pages. Then share your thoughts with another person this week.

CONTEMPLATE DEATH AND ETERNITY

Read Revelation 6:9-11 and then read the obituaries in today's newspaper. Say a prayer for the families, especially for any who seem not to have a church connection. Catch a sense of the tragedy of death, and pray for Jesus to return soon to restore life.

ENCOURAGE OTHERS

Do you know of a family that is struggling financially? Or a senior adult who just needs some company and conversation? Think about how you can meet their needs in a practical way. For example, you might want to purchase a grocery store gift certificate and send it to the family in financial difficulty.

Enclose a card with the words of Revelation 21:1-5, and include a personal note about how much you and Jesus care. (Or you might decide to give your gift anonymously, per Matthew 6:1-4.)

PRAY

Together, read out loud the prayers of Revelation 4:8, 11 and 5:12, 13.

BEFORE NEXT TIME: *The leader should e-mail or call group members to bring the following to the next session: editorial cartoons from a newspaper that include an easily recognizable symbol (such as a Republican elephant or the logo of a famous company); other images of (or actual) symbolic objects—either secular (such as an American eagle) or religious (such as a cross). The leader should also bring several of these. All group members should review "When You Feel You're at the End" by Jack Hayford (p. 67).*

Symbols | 3

Behind the sometimes mysterious imagery of Revelation
we find the promise of God's eternal faithfulness.

Revelation is written in an apocalyptic style. Apocalyptic literature (including parts of Daniel, Ezekiel, and Zechariah) was popular in the period between the Old and New Testaments and consists of two important characteristics.

The first characteristic is its message. *God spoke apocalyptic messages into desperate situations. Typically, the audience had experienced some form of oppression or persecution from a powerful enemy, and they felt hopeless. Into these circumstances, God offered a prophetic message confirming his sovereignty and promising to overthrow evil and establish justice. Believers were challenged to behave with renewed courage and devotion in light of God's promise of victory.*

The second characteristic of apocalyptic literature is its style. *An apocalyptic message usually appeared to a prophet as a vision or*

ΟΥΚΑΙΕΣΕΛΘΟΩΝΕΚΕΙΟΕΝΟΦΛΟΝΕ

dream. For that reason, the prophet communicated what he saw and heard, using rich imagery and unusual symbolism.

When we look at the symbols in Revelation, sometimes the meaning is clear; other times it's not. In either case, we can focus on what the text communicates about God's promises.

BIBLE BASIS: *Ezekiel 47:1-12; Revelation 13:1-17; 16:1-12, 17-21; 21:10-27; 22:1, 2*

EXTRA SUPPLIES: *editorial cartoons and symbolic objects*

 LAUNCH

Each member should hold one of the cartoons or symbolic objects that have been brought in. Write down a few words that describe your reaction to this symbol.

Then discuss these questions together:

- What does your symbol represent? Do you know how this symbol became associated with its meaning (for example, why an elephant represents a political party)?
- What feelings or gut reactions do you associate with your symbol? Why?
- Why do you think God gave us the book of Revelation filled with symbolism rather than more direct language?

❖ EXPLORE

Teaching Point One: The two beasts represent persecution.
Read Revelation 13:1-10.

The description of the first beast gives us clues about its purpose. Revelation 17:9, 10 tells us that the first beast's seven heads represent seven hills and seven kings. In the first century, Rome was known as "the city on seven hills." So the first beast likely represented the Roman Empire and its arrogant and violent emperors. Revelation 13:2, 3 describes the odd creature as having the body of a leopard, the feet of a bear, and the mouth of a lion.

What words or phrases indicate that this beast is trying to challenge God's authority or take his place?

What would be a symbol of persecution in your life?

Read Revelation 13:11-17.

The second beast performed signs and wonders and made people worship the first beast. This second beast likely represents emperor worship (an important aspect of Roman society in the first century) or, more generally, false religion. With his horns like a lamb, this beast is an imposter of Jesus, the perfect Lamb.

What aspects of life did these beasts control? What do these descriptions tell us about the environment first-century Christians were living in?

Do you know of any Christians who live under similar conditions of persecution today? Describe them.

Read "We Can Never Fear, Because Jesus Is Closer and More Powerful Than We Think" in "When You Feel You're at the End" by Jack Hayford (p. 73). How do John's descriptions of Jesus (as summarized by Hayford) contrast with the descriptions of the two beasts in Revelation 13?

Teaching Point Two: The seven bowls of God's wrath represent God's judgment of evil.
Read Revelation 16:1-12, 17-21.

God doesn't allow evil to reign forever. Instead, he exacts justice on the beasts and their followers. Interestingly, God's wrath is poured from bowls.

The Bible often speaks of God's wrath in language related to wine: it can be poured out (2 Chronicles 12:7; Psalm 69:24), served in a cup (Isaiah 51:17; Revelation 14:10), or consumed (Job 21:20). But these bowls call to mind the plagues God used against Egypt in Exodus 7–11 when that nation persecuted his people. God has been faithful in the past, and he will be faithful again.

Why do you think John wanted his readers to think of the Exodus story when they read Revelation? How are the situations similar? How are they different?

What were the results of the plagues in Egypt?

In Revelation 16:17-19, John reminded us that God's victory is certain. What other biblical scene does this passage remind you of? Do you think John was making a specific reference with these verses? If so, why?

How can believing in God's certain victory over evil influence the way you endure hardships in your own life?

Teaching Point Three: The new Jerusalem represents God's eternal presence with his people.

From the time of King David until AD 70, Jerusalem was at the center of Israel's hopes for a free and peaceable existence. David ruled from Jerusalem, and the temple built by his son Solomon was there. And it was in the temple that the Jews believed God's Spirit dwelled. Therefore, Jerusalem was a symbol of God's presence. When they were in exile, the Israelites often expressed their desire to be reunited to God, using language about the temple in Jerusalem (Psalm 42:4).

What place or experience do you associate closely with God's presence? Why?

In AD 70, Jerusalem and its temple were destroyed by the Romans—God's punishment for Israel's disobedience. Both the prophets and Jesus had foretold this event (Micah 3:12; Matthew 24:2). But God's people looked forward to a new Jerusalem where they would dwell with God forever.

Read Ezekiel 47:1-12; Revelation 21:10-27 and 22:1, 2.

Write down all the similarities you see between the descriptions of Jerusalem in Ezekiel and Revelation.

What image strikes you the most in both passages? Why do you think this image is important?

How can you experience God's presence in the midst of hardship?

 APPLY

This discussion about beasts and bowls and foreign cities might seem as if it has little to do with your daily life. But the message of Revelation is a call to live faithfully in light of God's faithfulness. Remember that God has promised to overthrow evil once and for all. In the meantime, we must remain committed to the gospel, to loving one another, and to loving our neighbors as ourselves.

Choose one of the following application options to do on your own this week. Turn to a partner and share your choice.

SYMBOL SEARCH

Choose a symbol from Revelation that your group didn't discuss—such as the seven seals, Babylon, "a new heaven and a new earth"—and research its possible meanings. Scan through the entire book of Revelation for clues. Also try to identify a Bible passage from outside of Revelation that helps explain the symbol.

IN HARM'S WAY

If your church supports a missionary or a mission field where Christians are currently facing persecution, do some research into the situation. Find out what obstacles those believers face and how you can pray for them. Then commit to pray for those believers every day this week—that they will have the courage to live out their faith boldly in the face of oppression.

TASTE OF HEAVEN

Spend thirty minutes this week in a church sanctuary, a park, or a quiet room in your house. Meditate on Revelation 21:10–22:5. Savor the beautiful language John uses to describe the Lord's presence with us in eternity. Then read Psalm 139:7-10 and Matthew 28:20 and thank him for being present with us both now and forever.

PRAY

Say this prayer aloud together: "God, we ask for courage as we await your final victory over sin. We are thankful for your presence here with us now, and we look forward to experiencing it fully when Christ returns. Until then, we pray with the apostle John, 'Amen. Come, Lord Jesus.'"

BEFORE NEXT TIME: *All members should search in newspapers, magazines, or online for stories of religious persecution around the world. Bring copies to the next meeting. (Voice of the Martyrs at www.persecution.com is a good source.) The leader should do the following: also obtain a number of persecution stories, borrow a CD of the "Hallelujah" chorus from Handel's* Messiah, *provide a CD player, make sure a whiteboard (or poster) and markers are available in the meeting area. All group members should read "Look, a Great White Horse!" by R. Geoffrey Brown (p. 85).*

Old Testament References | 4

Though the scenes and passion of John's revelation
are fresh and new, the images that shape the
book come largely from Old Testament writings.

Dragon. Whore of Babylon. Four horsemen. The images are so
memorable that they quickly remind us of the book of Revelation.
Indeed, few documents in history have been captured on canvas or
celluloid with the same intensity that has transformed the Apocalypse
into a literary and artistic genre of its own.

Although John's encounter with Jesus on the island of Patmos
produced a new revelation needed desperately by Christians under
persecution at the end of the first century, many of its themes and scenes
come directly from Old Testament books. John knew the language of
the Hebrew Bible and was attempting to describe events that had few
parallels. Only the prophetic anticipations of the past could shape
these powerful messages for the future. Reaching into the great exodus

from Egypt, the wonderful visions of Ezekiel, and the strange dreams of Daniel, John's record delivers a new word from God that grabs our imaginations and helps us see a world waiting to be born.

BIBLE BASIS: *Exodus 7–11; Ezekiel 2, 3; 47:1-12; Daniel 7:1-14; Revelation 1:9-18; 10; 15; 16; 22:1-5*

EXTRA SUPPLIES: *stories of religious persecution around the world, a CD of the "Hallelujah" chorus, CD player, a whiteboard (or poster) and markers*

 LAUNCH

Divide into groups of three or four people and look at the stories of persecution that each person brought. If necessary, divide the stories so that each smaller group has an equal number of stories. In your smaller group, briefly examine each story, using these questions:

- Was the persecution strictly religious, or was it state supported?
- Is it ongoing, or only a one-time incident?
- What was the local and international reaction to the incident?
- How did the people violated by the persecution react?

Come back together in the large group and share what might have caused some of the situations, what clashes of values might have come into play, and what both perpetrators and victims must have been feeling. Then discuss these questions:

When, where, and why have Christians been persecuted throughout history?

What sources of encouragement or hope seem to get Christians through times of persecution?

 EXPLORE

Teaching Point One: Daniel and Revelation have many parallels.
Read Daniel 7:1-14 and Revelation 1:9-18.

During various periods of Bible history, the defining theme for God's people was slavery, persecution, and foreign domination—such as Israel's years in Egypt between the patriarchs and the exodus. Later, Judah was absorbed into the Babylonian Empire, culminating with a period of deportation and exile. Next, it was the mighty Roman military machine that forced Judea into subservience. Finally, during John's later years, the Roman attack shifted from vanquishing the Jews to forcibly containing the Christians. During each dark epoch, God gave special revelation to his people, sustaining them in spirit even as they struggled against great physical oppression.

The prophet Daniel served as a key messenger of God's promises of hope during Judah's Babylonian exile. Through visions of approaching international and spiritual conflicts, Daniel delivered encouragement and a profound confidence in the future of God's kingdom, which always included the restoration of God's burdened and exploited people. The profound parallels between Daniel's visions in Daniel 7–12 and the scenes John described throughout Revelation can help us better understand what John was trying to communicate through his words.

As a group, list the similarities or parallels between what Daniel and John saw. What are the key themes in each vision?

What are the primary messages that these themes communicated to God's persecuted people in each historical setting?

The "son of man" designation (Daniel 7:13) is Daniel's term for the heavenly messenger who revealed the future of the people of God. Perhaps this is a theophany, a human appearance of God in Old Testament times to accommodate the people's inability to view the full glory of the transcendent Creator.

Of course, Jesus contains the fullness of God's glory within his human form, so that in New Testament times Jesus becomes the way that we best see God.

When John used the term "son of man" in Revelation 1:13, he seemed to indicate that Jesus, while completely at home in Heaven, is also fully in touch with those on earth whom God loves best. In what ways might we allow the "son

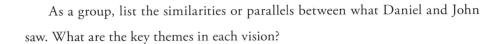

of man" as portrayed in verses 12-18 to impact us during times of tragedy and persecution?

Teaching Point Two: Revelation mirrors the book of Exodus in two distinct ways.

Read Revelation 15 and 16.

As we studied in session 2, John had a powerful vision of Jesus three different times (chapters 1, 5, and 19). Following each vision, Revelation contains different series of sevens. First there were the letters to the seven congregations in chapters 2, 3. Next came the opening of seven seals (anticipating the coming divine judgment), the blowing of seven trumpets (announcing the coming judgment), and the pouring of seven bowls of plagues in chapters 6–16 (accomplishing the divine judgment). And there is the description of seven things that will happen when Jesus returns to make all things new (Revelation 19:11–21:5).

As John tried to communicate what he saw in his visions, another display of divine wrath came to mind. John reached back to the beginning of Israel's history and drew on the mounting devastation produced at that time to find adequate descriptions of such judgment.

Skim Exodus 7–11, noting the ten plagues on Egypt. One member can write the key event of each disaster on a board or poster. What parallels can you find between the ten plagues on Egypt and the seven plagues in Revelation 16?

Why do you think certain plagues are repeated from one occasion to the other, and why were certain ones left out?

What was the point of the plagues on Egypt, and what's the intent of the plagues in the book of Revelation?

How were each of these expressions of divine anger a word of encouragement to the people of God experiencing persecution?

A second set of images from the book of Exodus finds a mirror image in the book of Revelation. The last half of Exodus is focused on the building of the tabernacle, a portable house of God where Yahweh would dwell among his people. This is also the theme in the final chapters of Revelation, where Heaven and earth merge and "the dwelling of God is with men" (Revelation 21:3). This is an amazing thought, both in the days of Israel and in the anticipations of the world still to come—the transcendent Creator chooses to take up residence, among all the corners of the vast and expanding universe, in our little neighborhood.

What do you think it will be like when God is so close that we can interact directly with him on a continuing basis?

How would this message bring hope and comfort to those in John's day who struggled under persecution? How does this teaching encourage you today?

Teaching Point Three: Ezekiel and Revelation both share a message of hope.
Read Ezekiel 2 and 3 and Revelation 10.

While the books of both Daniel and Exodus include scenes and images that find their way into the visions of Revelation, no Old Testament book contains as much of Revelation language and ideas as the prophecy of Ezekiel.

Ezekiel was born into a priest's family in Jerusalem in 622 BC, just as the province of Babylon began its eventually successful rebellion against the Assyrian kingdom.

Because King Josiah of Judah fought against the Egyptian division of the Assyrian alliance (Jeremiah 46:3-12), Babylon turned Judah into one of its territories, requiring payments of allegiance and carrying off promising young leaders like Daniel and his friends (Daniel 1). These men were to be trained in Babylonian religion, culture, history, and politics so that they could later be sent back to rule their home country on behalf of the conquerors.

Ezekiel was deported in 597 BC, during the next wave of Babylonian political adjustments. He was twenty-five at the time, the age at which he should have begun his apprenticeship as priest in the temple. Instead, he became a leader among the displaced exiles, couching his prophetic message in scenes powerfully shaped by the former (and future) temple back in Jerusalem.

What similarities do you see between Ezekiel and John regarding their willingness to speak on behalf of God?

Read Ezekiel 47:1-12 and Revelation 22:1-5.

The most dominant image that John repeated from Ezekiel's prophecy is the restoration of the earth. Ezekiel planted hope in the minds of the Jewish exiles that one day God would bring them back to Palestine and restore the glory of the region and the fortunes of the nation as the messianic age began. John saw similar images of the future when Jesus would return to make all things new. He placed these before his readers to provide hope to cling to during severe times of persecution.

What were Ezekiel and John trying to communicate through these pictures and symbols?

What message was God expressing about times yet to come? How would this message bring comfort and hope to those in Ezekiel's and John's days? How can you find comfort in this message when you feel challenged or persecuted?

Read the section "Christ's Future Victory Reinforces Our Endurance" in "Look, a Great White Horse!" by R. Geoffrey Brown (p. 90). How do you think you can experience the hope expressed in Brown's words and in Revelation 22 on a daily basis? Brainstorm with other members of your group.

APPLY

The message God issued through John in Revelation was one of comfort and hope for those under persecution. The repeated images and parallel scenes only reinforce the power of these booming declarations. Our task isn't just to read with interest, but also to share with confidence the hope they bring.

Choose one of the following application options to do on your own this week. Turn to a partner and share your choice.

BE AN ADVOCATE FOR THE PERSECUTED CHURCH

(This activity takes the "In Harm's Way" option from session 3 a step further.) Make a commitment to learn more about those parts of the global body of Christ that are hurting, despised, marginalized, and persecuted—especially any that your church supports. Do research to gain specifics. Then choose one particular area, region, or situation, and pledge to pray regularly and consistently for the power of Jesus to break through. You could raise awareness of their needs in congregational prayer networks. Or organize letter-writing campaigns to shower the missionaries with hope and encouragement. Write letters to government leaders who can make a difference.

SHARE HOPE WITH THE LOCALLY MARGINALIZED

Collaborate with your group to target one local group of people (such as those in hospitals, prisons, or retirement centers) who need regular reminders of Jesus' hope and encouragement. Choose passages from Revelation to read to those who are limited in their social mobility, and pray with them about the challenges they experience.

PAST AND FUTURE

The past speaks to the future. This week look at photos of your ancestors. Choose a few who were especially faithful believers. (If you do not come from a Christian family, consider some of your spiritual ancestors.) Note some admirable qualities each person possessed. E-mail this heritage information to some younger members of your extended family. Express thankfulness to God for these exemplary people from your past. Encourage family members to emulate their attributes and to pass the tradition along to future branches of your family tree.

 # PRAY

Listen together (and perhaps sing along!) to a recording of the "Hallelujah" chorus from Handel's *Messiah* as a closing prayer of confidence and testimony based upon the songs of Revelation.

BEFORE NEXT TIME: *Everyone should review "Look, a Great White Horse!" by R. Geoffrey Brown (p. 85).*

The Millennium | 5

The millennium is the kingdom of God in its fullness.

Throughout the Bible, the faithful looked forward to two epic events:
God's victory over evil and the just and peaceful reign of Christ.
For example, the prophets alluded to a time when "the wolf will live
with the lamb" (Isaiah 11:6); the apostles looked forward to ruling
with Jesus and "judging the twelve tribes of Israel" (Luke 22:30).
Revelation 20:1-7 gives these hopes a name—the "thousand years" (the
millennial kingdom)—and describes an era when Jesus will reign on
earth and Christians will live in peace and harmony with him as king.
But nowhere in Scripture outside of Revelation 20 is the millennium
discussed explicitly. For that reason, people disagree about what the
millennial reign will look like and when it will begin.

We will look at three perspectives on the millennium in this
session: premillennialism, postmillennialism, and amillennialism.
Keep in mind that the chronology and sequence of end-time events is

of secondary importance to the great gospel promise that Christ will one day rule on earth and Satan will be defeated. Although proponents of each of these perspectives understand this promise differently, they all take it seriously.

BIBLE BASIS: *Isaiah 2:2-4; Mark 4:30-32; John 5:28, 29; 2 Peter 3:8-14; Revelation 20:1-7*

EXTRA SUPPLIES: *none*

LAUNCH

As the group gathers, divide into pairs. Discuss these questions with your partner:

- If Jesus became president of the United States tomorrow, what would change? What, if anything, would remain the same?
- Do you think the world is a better place now than it was when Jesus first took on flesh in the first century? Is it a worse place? Explain your answer.

Come back together as the big group, where each pair can share a highlight of their discussion.

EXPLORE

Teaching Point One: Premillennialists believe that Jesus will return before the millennial reign.
Read Revelation 20:1-7.

Each of the views in the three teaching points is concerned with the relationship between the millennium and Christ's second coming. Premillennialism argues that Jesus will return before (*pre-*) the millennium. You might

IHϮΑΝΤΟΔΙΕϹШ°ᴴΠΟϷΕΥΟΜΕΝΟ

be familiar with this view because of the best-selling Left Behind fiction series by Tim LaHaye and Jerry Jenkins. Consistent with their perspective on the rest of Revelation, premillennialists take the sequence of events in Revelation 20 quite literally, seeing it as a road map of things to come.

Premillennialism stresses that the kingdom of God is not yet fully here. Although Jesus has won the victory over sin with his death on the cross, we won't know fully what the kingdom is like until Jesus returns. Life on earth will become increasingly harder until God finally intervenes by sending Jesus again.

Are you familiar with premillennialism as represented by the Left Behind series? What about those books struck you as helpful? What seemed odd to you?

In what ways do you see evidence that the kingdom of God is already among us? What would lead you to believe that it's not here completely?

Do you tend to interpret Revelation literally, as if it is a road map of the events that will occur at the end of human history? What influenced you to view Revelation the way you do?

Teaching Point Two: Postmillennialists believe that Jesus will return after the thousand-year reign of the kingdom.
Read Isaiah 2:2-4 and Mark 4:30-32.

Postmillennialists are more optimistic about human history than premillennialists are, because they tend to emphasize the present reality of the kingdom of God: "The time has come. . . . The kingdom of God is near" (Mark 1:15). They expect a steady progress of the gospel that will lead all nations to worship Christ, resulting in the millennial conditions described in Revelation 20. They believe the millennium might not be a literal thousand years, but Jesus will return after (*post-*) the millennium.

How do you understand the Parable of the Mustard Seed in Mark 4? Should conditions in the world change as the church worldwide grows larger?

How might your daily life be different if you emphasized the present reality of the kingdom rather than the future promise?

Postmillennialism reads Revelation less literally and more symbolically than premillennialism. Instead of understanding the book as a road map of the end, they believe it describes the end but that these events aren't necessarily in chronological order.

How does postmillennialism's less literal interpretation of Revelation strike you?

Teaching Point Three: Amillennialists believe in a figurative millennial reign of the kingdom on earth.
Read John 5:28, 29 and 2 Peter 3:8-14.

For amillennialists (literally, *no* millennium), the last days began when Jesus became flesh. That means he could return anytime and without warning. When he does, time as we understand it will end—we won't witness multiple stages in Christ's return. So the millennium described in Revelation 20 is not a literal thousand-year reign on earth. It's usually understood to be the period of time between Christ's first and second comings, however long that period of time may be in a literal sense. Christ is reigning now (as head of the church) over the living as well as the dead.

Instead of reading Revelation literally, amillennialists understand the book's symbolic language in light of the rest of the New Testament. As a result, they emphasize major themes and explain some of the details in different ways than do the proponents of the other views. Additionally, because they emphasize that Jesus' second coming will be sudden, they encourage believers to live godly and faithful lives in anticipation of Christ's return.

How do John 5:28, 29 and 2 Peter 3:8-14 describe Jesus' second coming?

Do you tend to believe Jesus' return will come without warning, or do you try to read the signs of the times? Why?

How might you act differently if you lived as if Jesus could return at any moment?

Write down one thing about each of the three views that you find helpful and one thing you find confusing or questionable.

In "Look, a Great White Horse!" R. Geoffrey Brown says:

This vision of victory is necessary for our hope, faith, and endurance. Because we live in an age where we see far too much, we see far too little. But what we do see sometimes seems so strong that it makes our faith seem weak. So, in a sense, we must have this vitamin supplement of the book of Revelation, where we clearly see the triumph of the truth and the principles that are spoken of throughout the Bible. In Revelation, we see the arc that spans the stormy history of the ages. We listen to thunder rolls on the last great day when the kingdoms of this world become the kingdom of our Lord and his Christ. Resplendent with glory, it makes the brightest day in human history look like midnight. It makes our sufferings—I don't want to make light of them—pale in significance before the triumph and the glories to be revealed (p. 87).

In light of that paragraph, what do all three of the perspectives have in common?

What suffering are you experiencing right now? Often we hear the advice to live one day at a time through our trials. Brown seems to encourage us to look ahead to the "triumph and glories" of eternity. How can you follow this guidance in the midst of your own trials and sufferings?

 APPLY

Debates about issues such as the timing of the millennium can easily distract us from the beautiful promise of Revelation: that Christ will one day reign over his people in peace and justice. That promise is the fulfillment of his kingdom—a kingdom that has already come, if only in part. Knowing when that promise is going to be fulfilled is far less important than living in the confidence that God is always faithful to keep his word. Perhaps that's why some believers claim simply to be *pan*millennialists—trusting that it's all going to pan out. And others call themselves *pro*millennialists—whatever God wants to do, they're for it! This week, make a special effort to live as a citizen of God's kingdom in the present.

How does this great theme of Revelation—that Christ will one day reign over his people in peace and justice—affect your daily life?

How can you live more fully in light of that promise? Brainstorm with your group to list practical ways to live out his promise each day.

Choose one of the following application options to do on your own this week. Turn to a partner and share your choice.

DIG DEEPER

Refer back to the notes you made about the three views on the millennium—what you found most helpful and what you found most troubling. Using resources from your church, your local library, or the Internet, explore in greater depth the perspective you find most compelling. Look specifically for answers to any questions or concerns this study raised but did not address completely. E-mail or call someone in your group to share what you learn.

KEEP A JOURNAL

As you interact with your coworkers, neighbors, and family this week, keep in mind the possibility that Jesus could return at any moment. At the end of each day, write down a brief description of how your behavior in certain situations might have been different if you were more conscious of the immediacy of Jesus' return.

EMBRACE THE MILLENNIUM

You don't have to wait for the millennium to serve Christ the king. As you read or watch the news, interact with those in your home, and choose entertainment, try to determine whether you think of the kingdom more in terms of "already" or "not yet." Keep track of the evidences that the kingdom is a present reality. Each day this week, pray the Lord's Prayer (Matthew 6:9-13). As you do, consider how you can contribute to God's will being done on earth as it is in Heaven.

 PRAY

Pray together that you will live in the confidence that Jesus is returning and will one day reign in peace over all the earth. Ask God to show you specifically how he wants you to live out the promise of his kingdom. If he brings specific ideas to mind, be sure to make notes here or in a journal.

BEFORE NEXT TIME: *The leader should search newspapers, magazines, or the Internet for current or historical political cartoons that can be easily read and understood by the members of your group. Photocopy or print out the cartoons in an enlarged format so all participants can see them at the same time. Group members should review "Look, a Great White Horse!" by R. Geoffrey Brown (p. 85).*

Relevance | 6

Revelation should dramatically impact our daily lives.

Locusts that look like horses with human faces, a sea of glass mixed with fire, frog-ish evil spirits exiting the mouth of a dragon . . . Revelation can be very interesting. But how can we actually apply the words of Revelation to our daily lives? Besides reading Revelation as some sort of Christianized Nostradamus, how can we allow this urgently written letter to affect our choices, relationships, and theology?

In Revelation 1:3 we read, "Blessed is he who reads and those who hear the words of the prophecy, and heed the things which are written in it; for the time is near" (NASB, emphasis added). The verse is also rendered, "How blessed the reader! How blessed the hearers and keepers of these oracle words, all the words written in this book!" (The Message, emphasis added). Revelation isn't just a telescope into the future. Revelation is a book to be obeyed. So how do we obey Revelation?

IH†ΛΝΤΟΔΙΕϹШΟΝΠΟΓΕΥΟΜΕΝΟΙ

BIBLE BASIS: *Revelation 1:9-20; 3:1-6, 14-22; 11:15-19; 14:6, 7; 19:1-11; 22:7-10*

EXTRA SUPPLIES: *political cartoons*

BEFOREHAND: *The leader may want to recruit a reader for "Teaching Point Two."*

LAUNCH

As your group leader holds up the political cartoons one at a time, discuss the following questions for each cartoon:

- What sort of imagery exists in this cartoon? What represents what?
- Is there a call to action from this cartoon? What is the cartoonist telling you, a political leader, or a government organization to do? How does the cartoon reveal the mind-set, bias, or ideology of the artist?

In *Discipleship on the Edge*, Darrell Johnson writes about how New Testament scholar George Beasley-Murray compares the imagery used in Revelation to contemporary imagery in political cartoons. "He does not mean to be sacrilegious in his suggestion," Johnson writes, "and he fully recognizes that the images are more than political cartoons. He is helping us understand how imagery works on the imagination—both for individuals and for groups like empires and nations" (Regent College Publishing, 2004, p. 36).

EXPLORE

Teaching Point One: Revelation calls us out of complacency.
Read Revelation 3:1-6.

In these verses, we read the letter to the church of Sardis. This church was active, organized, had sound doctrine, and was the largest congregation of all the seven churches. Yet they were accused of being dead. *The Message* gives verses 1, 2 as: "I see right through your work. You have a reputation for vigor and zest, but you're dead, stone dead. Up on your feet! Take a deep breath! Maybe there's life in you yet. But I wouldn't know it by looking at your busywork; nothing of God's work has been completed."

Is it possible to carry out a spiritual task or discipline while totally missing the point? How does this happen in churches now?

In *Discipleship on the Edge*, Darrell Johnson points out that "this church had silently accommodated itself to the injustice and immorality of the city. In particular, it had silently accommodated itself to the sexual morés of the city" (p. 98). How does silent complacency regarding sexual morés affect the church today? What are subtle ways the church has bought into sexual norms of today's culture? How do you think we could remedy this?

In this text, Jesus gives the church several commands. What are they, and how can you apply them directly to your life?

Read Revelation 3:14-22.

The final letter to the seven churches was the most inviting. "Here I am!" Jesus says. "I stand at the door and knock." He's not talking to unbelievers. Jesus is talking to believers—believers who are, as he describes, "lukewarm."

What were the promises and warnings in this letter?

In *Discipleship on the Edge*, Darrell Johnson notes that "lukewarmness is caused by compromise." He continues: "The disciples of Jesus in the first century were under tremendous pressure to compromise with the so-called 'imperial cult': to not only swear allegiance to Caesar as god, but to then live by the values and priorities of the idolatrous empire. The disciples in Laodicea had apparently succumbed to the pressure. They had developed a brand of Christianity to live in relationship with Jesus in the private, religious realm, and then live the values and priorities of Rome in the public, secular realm" (p. 21).

As part of the church today, how do we succumb to lukewarmness? In what ways do we live two lives like the Laodiceans? How can we counteract this?

Teaching Point Two: Revelation teaches us to worship only Christ.

One person can read aloud Revelation 1:9-20 while the other participants close their eyes and listen to John's vision.

What sorts of images came to mind? How do they compare and contrast to the usual picture of Christ from the Gospels? How do these words change your vision of Christ?

How can you respond in worship to Christ as he's portrayed in this passage?

Read Revelation 14:6, 7; 19:9-11 and 22:7-10.

Both of the times John bowed to an angel, the angel said almost identical words: "Do not do it! I am a fellow servant with you and with your brothers who hold to the testimony of Jesus. Worship God!" (19:10). Why did John bow down at the feet of an angel? How does humanity usually respond in the face of awe? How much of worship is a result of fear?

What can we learn from John's worship experiences during the revelation of Christ?

Describe a profound worship experience you've had. What set that experience apart from other times of worship? Why is worship so important in our relationship with Christ? What are some ways that your daily life can be characterized by this kind of worship?

Teaching Point Three: Revelation teaches us to hope in nothing but Jesus. Read Revelation 11:15-19 and 19:1-8.

These are just two of the hymns to Christ in Revelation, expressing worship for the great things he has done and expressing hope for what he is yet to do. What actions was Christ being praised for in these hymns?

The Message version of Revelation 11:15 states: "The kingdom of the world is now the Kingdom of our God and his Messiah! He will rule forever and ever!" Often we find it easy to *say* that Jesus is the King of kings and Lord of lords. Yet because we hear it so much, perhaps we forget what it actually means.

If you truly acted on your belief that Jesus is the king, how would it affect the way you respond to other powers in the world: economics, politics, and culture? How would it affect the way you respond to friends, neighbors, and family members?

Read the paragraph about Julian's army in "Look, a Great White Horse!" by R. Geoffrey Brown (p. 90). Christ has already overcome, continues to overcome, and *will* overcome! Our worries and concerns about today, while legitimate, are no cause for despair, because Christ is already king! Not in the future, not after traumatic worldly and heavenly events, but now!

Any human being or ideology claiming to bring hope, claiming to have the solution, claiming to rescue us from sin or its consequences is false. Christ has already done this!

In what circumstances have you forgotten or been tempted to forget that Christ is already king over all? In what false powers have you placed hope?

How can you serve Christ as king in your daily life? In what specific ways should acknowledging him as king change the way you live?

 APPLY

One of the very first verses in Revelation says we'll be blessed if we obey the words of the book. Then clearly we can experience those blessings now. How? By taking true action—not busywork—to do God's will and work; by sincerely and constantly worshiping God; and by claiming the promise of hope in Christ, who is already victorious.

Choose one of the following application options to do on your own this week. Turn to a partner and share your choice.

TAKE A BREAK AND TAKE ACTION

Is your life so busy that you go through spiritual motions without awareness of their ultimate meaning? If so, take a one-day break. Take a day off work, turn off your phone, shut down your computer, hire someone to watch your children if necessary, and consider Revelation 3:1-6 as a letter written to you. Read it aloud, meditate on it, and consider how you might be metaphorically dead. Note some ways to "rise again." Pray for God's help.

WORSHIP GOD EVERYWHERE

Today you read how John—the close friend and follower of Christ—bowed down to worship an angel. If *he* accidentally worshiped the wrong thing, how much easier is it for us to misplace our worship! Slowly walk through your home and workplace. Where are places you forget to worship Christ? What are items or examples of your own misplaced worship? If you find places or items that lead you astray, change. Change the space, throw away items that lead you astray. Renovate surroundings to consistently invite you to worship God.

WHERE'S YOUR HOPE?

Most people have a tendency to misplace their hope. Many in our society trust in the economy, physical health, and the government or other established organizations. In your journal or this book, list ways you misplace your hope. Then look for opportunities to change your actions or speaking based on your realization of misplaced hope. For example, perhaps you credit recent physical healing to treatments or a healthy diet. Instead, give credit to God for creating both bodies that heal and resources (food and drugs) that help heal them.

 PRAY

During this time of prayer, move into a traditional posture of worship: completely bowed down, just as John would have been before Christ. Take turns praying aloud, focusing on confessing complacency while acknowledging to Christ his kingship, power, and the hope you have only in him.

BEFORE NEXT TIME: *Because this is the final study session in* Crash Course on Revelation, *the group might want to meet once more for fellowship and food and to spend time together celebrating the completion of this course. Members could scan the six sessions in this book before the get-together in order to find the most meaningful or life-changing thing they've gained from your study together. Then close the celebration with group members sharing that personal point. In addition, if your group plans to continue studying together, consider what Bible subject you want to tackle next. If you like the approach of this Crash Course study, check out www.standardpub.com for other titles in the series.*

FOR FURTHER RESEARCH

Note: The Crash Course series is designed to help you study important topics easily. The following books and magazine articles present additional valuable research. Items in the resource list are provided as a starting point for digging even deeper. Not everything in "For Further Research" is necessarily written from a conservative evangelical viewpoint. Great discussion and real learning happen when a variety of perspectives are examined in light of Scripture. We recommend that you keep a concordance and Bible dictionary nearby to enable you to quickly find Bible answers to any questions.

RESOURCE LIST

Revelation, Leon Morris, (The Tyndale New Testament Commentaries series, Eerdmans, 1987; InterVarsity Press, 2007). This commentary is the result of top-level scholarly work, yet doesn't get weighed down with advanced, technical terminology.

The Meaning of the Millennium, Robert Clouse (InterVarsity Press, 1977). This book brings together proponents of four different views on the millennium connected with Christ's return. After each view is presented, the proponents of the competing views respond from their perspectives.

What Christ Thinks of the Church: An Exposition of Revelation 1–3, John R. W. Stott (Baker, 2003). Stott explores the first three chapters of Revelation—particularly the letters to seven churches of the ancient world—to uncover the message and insights these letters hold for the church today.

The Throne, the Lamb and the Dragon: A Reader's Guide to the Book of Revelation, Paul Spilsbury (InterVarsity Press, 2002). This author uses the symbolism in Revelation to present a view of the book not as one filled with detailed prophecy but a book where the symbols stand for the church age and the struggles all Christians face.

Revelation As Drama, James L. Blevins (B&H Publishing Group, 1984). This book takes the task of literary and historical analysis of Revelation and makes it accessible to readers of all levels.

The Book of Revelation, Harry R. Boer (Eerdmans, 1979). This relatively short book provides a concise introduction of Revelation, a brief commentary on each chapter, and concludes with a "Meaning for Today" section. The author, who was a missionary in Nigeria, writes largely without a Western slant.

More Than Conquerors: An Interpretation of the Book of Revelation, William Hendriksen (Baker, 1998; originally written in 1939). Hendricksen focuses on a study of the time when Revelation was written, as well as what it would have meant to its original audience.

Revelation and the End of All Things, Craig R. Koester (Eerdmans, 2001). This guide to Revelation deals with many questions people most often ask about this difficult book of the Bible, striking a balance between the first-century context and Revelation's relevance to twenty-first-century readers.

The Book of Revelation (New International Commentary on the New Testament series, Robert H. Mounce, Eerdmans, 1997). In this book, the author aims to keep the message of Revelation in the forefront, boiling down sometimes complex arguments of various views to a few sentences that make sense.

The Lion and the Lamb: A Commentary on the Book of Revelation for Today, John Newport (B&H Publishing Group, 1998). Covers the various methods of interpreting Revelation, quoting other authors on Revelation and providing short essays on important topics in the book.

The Message of Revelation, Michael Wilcock (InterVarsity Press, 1991). Not intended to be a complete commentary on Revelation, this book instead looks at the drama of Revelation in eight scenes.

Revelation, Grant R. Osborne (Baker Exegetical Commentary on the New Testament series, Baker Academic, 2002). This commentary aims to interpret the text of Revelation while also exploring the perspectives of contemporary scholarship. Rather than looking at each verse in depth, the author examines larger sections to emphasize the central message and theology of Revelation.

When You Feel You're at the End

Whatever our circumstances, we must see that Jesus is here.

by Jack Hayford

My wife, Anna, and I have a collection of pictures taken of us with fairly well-known people. We've intentionally placed these photos in a rather inconspicuous location because it could seem disgustingly ostentatious to our friends to have these pictures of Jack and Anna with famous people pushed in their faces.

We also have five framed letters from three U.S. presidents and two others most people would know. These personal letters are real treasures.

The book of Revelation is a personal letter from Jesus to his church. What could be more treasured than a letter from Jesus?

This letter opens the revelation of Jesus Christ, which God gave to his servants. I'm a servant to Jesus, so it's a letter to me. He sent it by his angels through his servant John, who serves as the stenographer taking the letter and the mailman delivering the letter.

The Lord approached John where he was, providing a picture of circumstances so much like ours that we can completely identify with him. While Revelation shows much of the character and person of Jesus, it remains a personal letter. That's important to fix in our minds because it's going to be a great challenge for us to capture the prophetic significance of the book and gain the personal implications for our lives.

The book of Revelation often becomes an object of sensation or speculation. Jesus was not writing to his people to tell them: *Here's a whole bunch of stuff you can guess about until I come again. It will be fun to try and figure out which chart is right.* More likely he said: *I want to tell you things that will help make your life work in the middle of a world that holds every kind of challenge you can imagine. And I want you to see the victory! I want you to know that I'm there when you feel you're at the end—whether it's the end of time or the end of your rope.*

Revelation 1 gives the reason that Jesus reveals himself. It's not a revelation of information; it's a revelation of Jesus. It's not a revelation of prophecy; it's a revelation of Jesus: "The revelation of Jesus Christ, which God gave him to show his servants" (Revelation 1:1). The book of Revelation is *of* Jesus and *from* him. The traits of his person are manifest in a marvelous vision John records at the beginning, because we're looking at Jesus.

As we study the whole book of Revelation, our perspective can easily become disjointed. When you mention Revelation, you're less likely to have someone say to you, "What did you capture of new things about Jesus in that book?" than you are for someone to say, "What do you think 666 really is? And who are the two witnesses? And when is the rapture going to occur?"

The reason Jesus reveals himself is to help us keep things in perspective. Why? Because "the time is near" (Revelation 1:3).

We read those words and think, *Well, I believe Jesus is coming soon, but he wrote those words 1,920 years ago, and John thought he was coming. He didn't come then. Paul thought he was coming; didn't come then. People in the last generation thought he was coming. I think he's coming. In fact, I really feel he is coming in my life, but who knows.*

To keep things in perspective the Lord wants us to gain a view from heaven. Life lived in the continuum will stampede and distress you when pressure comes.

This week Anna and I prayed with a young woman whose husband is about to trash his family for no reason other than a horrific entrapment—emotionally and mentally—with someone he met on the Internet. This situation is characteristic of the insanity of our time.

Also this week, a couple in our church got the message that one member of their family murdered another member of the family. There was no logical explanation. There never is for murder. It exploded out of nowhere and burst upon the family.

And this week, I heard from a friend who launched upon a project with all his heart, and the thing collapsed right under him. When he reexamined things closely, he discovered that a foolish oversight on his part was the cause.

A young woman whose husband is about to ruin their home. A couple facing a murder in their family. A man with the collapse of a great vision. Things happen—we face them all the time—when you feel you're at the end.

Yet whatever you're going through is brief in comparison to what your life is ultimately about. Your life isn't about your present financial or domestic stress. I'm not suggesting that we should be passive about life's realities. I'm not suggesting the Lord is indifferent toward our problems. He's saying: *I want you to see me and to see that whatever you're going through is not what your life is ultimately about.* He wants us to keep things in perspective.

He comes to say: *I'm committed to seeing you through it all.* "Blessed is the one who reads the words" (Revelation 1:3). He says: *You want a blessing? Keep reading this often. Stay in this book, and it will keep your eyes above it all.*

He says: *I have signed it myself.* The signature of Jesus on the book of Revelation is of no small significance. He's saying: *This is personal to you, and I'm endorsing everything I've said here.*

He says: *I want you to rest your life on this, and I am the life giver. I will support you. I am the resurrected one, the first and the last. Death can't keep me down, and when you come to the end it can't keep you down either. I'm going to see you through it all. I made you kings and priests unto God. There's a promise of dominion as long as we walk in worship. Kings who war with victory; priests who through their worship draw the authority to function as kings.*

The content of the message proceeds from here. In Revelation 1:9-20, John describes an encounter that gives us the message Jesus reveals. This message includes six assurances to us whenever we feel we're at the end.

WE CAN NEVER BE IN A PLACE WHERE CHRIST'S LOVE WON'T FIND US

The first assurance we derive from the words "I, John . . . was on the island called Patmos" (Revelation 1:9, *NASB*). John was on Patmos because he was under persecution by the Roman government.

There's something particularly significant about his words "the island called Patmos." Patmos was not a known place. I was on a cruise with a group of believers and we went to Patmos, a Greek island in the Aegean Sea. It's just a dot on the face of this planet, and in John's time, it was a Roman penal colony. The island is less than four miles square.

While this island has become famous to us, and present-day cruise ships stop there because it's a nice port and an interesting stop in the Aegean, people in John's day didn't really know about Patmos. So he used the terminology "the island *called* Patmos." If you're traveling and someone asks, "Where do you live?" you wouldn't say, "I live in a place called Los Angeles." You'd say, "I live in Los

Angeles," because it's known. However, if you were from a small, rural town in Montana, you might say, "I live in a place called Simpson, in north central Montana near the Canadian border."

What's important here is that Jesus visited John where he was. John isn't just recording interesting information. This message is important because the Lord Jesus was saying: *You can never be in so forsaken a place my love won't seek and find you.* That's the heart of his message.

You might feel you're in a place called confusion or despair, or that you're isolated on an island called rejection. But John is reporting the revelation of Jesus Christ, saying, *Jesus came to me when I was on an island off in the middle of nowhere.*

WE CAN NEVER BE SO BOUND THAT THE SPIRIT CAN'T LIFT OUR SOUL WITH HOPE

In Revelation 1:10, John writes, "On the Lord's Day I was in the Spirit, and I heard behind me a loud voice like a trumpet."

John wasn't just physically in a penal colony, he was also under the scepter of the world's imperial power of that time, Rome. There's no escape. There's no circumstance that can alter his situation. He is under the heel of Roman power. He says: *I was there at the end of the world and at the end of anything I could do, with no way out. But on this day I transcended that. I went into the Spirit on the Lord's Day. I might have been on Patmos, but I want to tell you about a day I got in the Spirit.*

Whenever you feel you're at the end, you can identify your surroundings and think, *These are the limits.* Or you can transcend those limits by saying, "Father God, I come to begin to worship you and get in the Spirit." That will begin to transcend any circumstance you're in. It's not a matter of happy talk. It's not a matter of good feelings. It's to move into the realm of the Spirit through worship.

There are two ways to interpret the phrase "on the Lord's Day." John is probably referring to both.

First, "on the Lord's Day" refers to the first day of the week. It's called the Lord's Day because Jesus sanctified the first day of the week with his resurrection. So John might have received this vision on a Sunday and he says, "I was in the Spirit."

Second, "on the Lord's Day" also reflects the day of God's judgment and visitation—the day that he comes to crush his enemies and to release his own. In the book of Revelation, John will capture a vision of that eventual entry of God's delivering power over this whole planet and of his people.

John is saying what Jesus wants us to see in this: *You can never be so bound that my Spirit can't lift your soul with hope. Got a problem? Get in the Spirit.*

WE CAN NEVER LOSE WHEN JESUS WRITES THE END OF OUR STORY

John tells us that he heard a voice saying, "I am the Alpha and the Omega. . . . I am the First and the Last. . . . Write, therefore, what you have seen, what is now and what will take place later" (Revelation 1:8, 17, 19). Jesus tells John to address the book to the congregations that had been John's scope of oversight.

Alpha and Omega are the A and the Z of the Greek alphabet. Jesus says: *I am Alpha and Omega, the First and the Last. The One who is, who was, and who is to come.*

The Message translates this as follows: "I'm A to Z. I'm The God Who Is, The God Who Was, and The God About to Arrive. I'm the Sovereign-Strong" (Revelation 1:8). Jesus is making a statement: History can't be written until Jesus has the last word.

He's saying: *I am here as the one who is the beginning. I'm the author and the finisher of your faith. I am the Creator, the consummator of all things. Between the*

creation and the consummation I am the Redeemer of whatever you're going through.
I am the A to Z, the first to last, and wherever you are in the middle of what seems
like the end, it's not the end of the story yet. I'm going to write the end of your story. I'm
going to write it my way no matter what the circumstance is, and you're not the loser.

John isn't saying: *I had a personal visit from Jesus and I'm here at this local*
Christian banquet to tell you how I, the apostle, heard from God. To the contrary,
in Revelation 1:9 John says: I'm "John, your brother and companion in the suffering and kingdom and patient endurance that are ours in Jesus." He seems to
be saying: *We go through tough stuff together, and I'm another member of the family,*
and I want to tell you how Jesus treats the members of the family.

The only logic for his reporting this is to let us know the way Jesus reveals
himself and what it's intended to mean to us.

WE CAN NEVER FEAR, BECAUSE JESUS IS CLOSER AND MORE POWERFUL THAN WE THINK

As John writes the words of Revelation 1:10-18 and describes this encounter
with Jesus, sixty years have gone by since the last time he saw Jesus personally on
the Mount of Olives in the year AD 30.

Suddenly, John said, *I heard a voice that sounded like a blast from a trumpet*
and I turned around. John sees the splendor of the majesty of the reigning Christ,
who at the right hand of the throne of all power above is the Lord of all. Words
seem to fail him. He labors to come up with a description: *eyes like fire.* He says:
Oh, if you could have seen the way his hair was.

With a sense of the majesty of the Savior, John said, "I fell at his feet as though
dead" (v. 17). Then the Lord spoke: "I am the Living One; I was dead, and behold I
am alive for ever and ever! And I hold the keys of death and Hades" (v. 18).

There's a great significance in this encounter, because no one knew Jesus
any better than John. He was the closest friend to the Savior during his earthly

ministry. This most familiar person turns to see Jesus and is overwhelmed. In this message of Jesus, when we face times that we think we're at the end, I hear him say to those of us who know him well: *You might think you know me well, but you haven't seen anything yet.*

Hallelujah!

When Jesus calls you in the midst of your circumstance—when you feel you're at the end—you can lift up your head a little higher because he says: *I'm more powerful than you think, and I'm closer than you think.*

WE CAN NEVER FACE ANYTHING GOD'S POWER CAN'T TAKE US THROUGH

We need to note another statement from Revelation 1: "His feet were like bronze glowing in a furnace" (v. 15). The feet of Christ—once wounded—have become feet of dominion. The figure of bronze in Scripture denotes strength. As the metal was worked, the tempering effect of the fire allowed it to be shaped into formidable shields or other implements of protection for warfare. Bronze gates describe the defense of a city. Nothing depicts strength more than the concept of bronze being fired in the furnace. Imagine, perhaps the last thing John saw in this vision of Jesus—the last thing noticeable as he disappeared—were the feet that had been pierced. John sees these feet as having a bronze quality. They're not bronze feet; they're feet that appear as bronze.

There's a glory and an authority that the Savior who sits on the throne—all principalities and powers under his feet—has called us to: to completeness in him, to a place seated and secured in Christ. He says: *As you find your security in me, then those feet begin to manifest through you. Whatever the attacks of the adversary, you'll crush the serpents and the scorpions under your feet.*

Walk in the trail of the One who has gone through the fire. When you go through the fire, as he did, you discover what he found going through it.

I was speaking with a young pastor who was facing tremendous difficulty because he felt forsaken. I urged him to rest his case with the Lord. He wasn't angry at God. But he felt that he couldn't trust God. I reminded him of Jesus saying, "My God, my God, why have you forsaken me?" (Mark 15:34). Then, only a few moments later saying, "Father, into your hands I commit my spirit" (Luke 23:46). In this moment of Christ's greatest sense of aloneness came the moment of his greatest placing of trust and rest in the Father.

When we go through the fires, no matter what causes us to say, "I'm at the end and God's not even around in this situation anymore," the Lord says to us: *If you'll abandon yourself and trust me, then you will go through that fire and you will find a pathway of dominion like my Son's. There is nothing you face that is unanticipated by my plan or unsurpassed by my power.*

That's what the Savior went through at the cross. The Father's plan and the Father's power brought him through, and he says: *That's how my feet got this way. I want you to walk with me and learn the same thing—there is never a plan to disregard or neglect you. No matter how alone or confused you seem in the midst of life, my plan transcends it and my power will take you through it.*

WE CAN NEVER BE LOST, BECAUSE JESUS HOLDS US IN HIS HAND

We come to the final point. In John's vision he sees the right hand of the Savior. In his right hand were stars, and these stars were people. Not stars in terms of famous personalities. They were stars in the sense of the radiance that is invested in people of the kingdom of God—a radiance intended to light the darkness of the world. The apostle Paul said: "Do everything without complaining or arguing, so that you may become blameless and pure, children of God without fault in a crooked and depraved generation, in which you shine like stars in the universe" (Philippians 2:14, 15).

When John sees Christ's hand with the stars, he realizes that this same hand reaches over to him. Just when Jesus seems to be out of reach to us, he says: *I have you firmly in hand.*

Revelation reminds us that we're in the hands of the Savior. Whether it's the end of time or you just find yourself at the end of your rope, the Savior says: *I'm here. I'm here no matter how remote you seem to yourself, out of touch. No matter what you think I may have been like in times past, you ain't seen nothing yet. I'm here in the middle of your circumstance to put my hand on you, to show my glorious power, to walk you through the fire. I'm here. I've come to show you that compared to what your life is ultimately about, this is only a brief time. I'm going to take you through it.*

The Gift of Vision

If we are to grow, we must focus upon the
Lamb who was slain.

We all have a frame of reference through which we look out at the world. These glasses weren't given to us by an optician. We received them from our parents and extended family, our childhood experiences, our school teachers, and our culture. These glasses affect everything about our life. . . .

Now, whether or not we can fully articulate these basic presuppositions, we have them. They're revealed in the decisions we make every day: the way we treat people, the way we react to the news, and the way we spend our time and our money. You wouldn't ever have to speak; I could follow you around for a week with a video camera, and then play back that video. Just from watching you, I could deduce your basic presuppositions about life. Those basic presuppositions determine everything about us. If we are to change and grow, there must be a change in the basic vision, framework, and presuppositions that we hold.

Revelation 5 gives us distinctively Christian glasses. This set of glasses clarifies our view of earth as nothing else does. What do we see when we look through Revelation 5 glasses? It's so thrilling! I've often wondered how the eighty-year-old apostle John handled this vision. His little old heart must have been pounding; he must have been wondering if he was going to make it.

GOD IS IN CONTROL AND HIS PLAN IS SECURE

In Revelation 5, the camera zooms in on the right hand of the One who sits on the throne. John sees a scroll held firmly by that hand. It's clearly a book of crucial, unparalleled importance. It overflows to the extent that it's written on both the inside and the outside. It's sealed with seven seals to ensure the safety of its decree.

The scroll contains the meaning of history—the meaning of world history, but also the meaning of your history and my history. The image of the scroll in the hand of God underscores the message of Revelation 4—that God is in control. The fact that there is a scroll says that there is order behind the chaos, that there is a plan, and that the plan is secure because it is held tightly in the right hand of the Almighty.

Then John sees a mighty angel, a strong creature of that other dimension. The angel shouts out in a loud voice. The voice needs to be loud because the call is being sent out to the far reaches of the universe. In a loud voice he says, "Who is worthy to break the seals and open the scroll?" (Revelation 5:2). We can echo that question. Who indeed? Who is worthy to open the plan of history and then bring history to its foreordained consummation? John then is hit with the devastating truth: No one is able. No one was found worthy of that supreme task. No one on the earth, no one under the earth, no one in heaven can come before the throne and take the scroll from him who holds it so tightly.

No one. This is a very humbling admission. We can make spaceships and land men on the moon. We can create and assemble intricate and complex electronic systems. We can write beautiful poetry. We can paint beautiful pictures. We can conceive and beget babies. But none of us can discover and then implement the secret of history. The scroll is sealed by the Almighty, and having searched the whole universe over, no one was found who had the power or wisdom or moral excellence to break its seals. John said, "I wept and wept" (Revelation 5:4).

Then comes the very heart of the Christian vision of reality. Let the imagery of this vision sink into your imagination, and let it explode in your emotions and your intellect. Oh, I want so badly for you to see this, and for it to grab hold of you. The elder speaks to John, and John turns his gaze away from the throne to this elder. The elder says to him, "Do not weep! See, the Lion of the tribe of Judah, the Root of David, has triumphed. He is able to open the scroll" (Revelation 5:5).

The images of the Lion of Judah and the Root of David were present in the messianic expectation. The Lion of the tribe of Judah comes from Genesis 49:9, where Judah is described as a lion's cub. And the image of the Root of David comes from Isaiah 11, a passage we love to read at Christmastime: "A shoot will come up from the stump of Jesse [David's father]; from his roots a Branch will bear fruit" (v. 1). When this Root comes, "with justice he will give decisions for the poor of the earth. . . . The wolf will live with the lamb, the leopard will lie down with the goat. . . . The earth will be full of the knowledge of the LORD as the waters cover the sea" (vv. 4, 6, 9).

Then John turns his gaze from the angel back to the throne. Are you ready for this? This is the key transition of the vision. John turns, expecting to see what? A roaring lion. But: "I saw a Lamb, looking as if it had been slain, standing in the center of the throne. . . . And they sang a new song: 'You are worthy to take the scroll and to open its seals. . . . Worthy is the Lamb, who was slain, to receive power'" (Revelation 5:6, 9, 12).

There are two words for *lamb* in Greek. The more usual word is the word *amnos,* and it means "adult lamb." It is the word John the Baptist used when he saw Jesus of Nazareth and said, "Look, the Lamb of God, who takes away the sin of the world!" (John 1:29). But there's another word, *amion*. It means "little lamb," and that's the word John uses in this scene. "The Lion of the tribe of Judah . . . has triumphed. . . . Then I saw a [little lamb]" (Revelation 5:5, 6). Mary's little Lamb. Let this image grab you. The Lamb has seven eyes and seven horns. What did this convey? Eyes are the picture of wisdom; seven is the number of completeness and essence. The little Lamb is immensely wise. Horns are the picture of strength, and there are seven of them, so this little Lamb is immensely powerful. The little Lamb is the perfection and the essence of the power and wisdom of God. . . .

The conquering Lamb wins via the cross. The Lion overcomes by becoming the sacrificial Lamb. Let the image sink in.

I want you to notice one more thing before I draw some observations from this. This little Lamb was standing in the very center of the four living creatures, which means that Jesus Christ is the center of creation. In the very center of the twenty-four elders, which means that Jesus Christ is the very center of redeemed humanity, the church. What's interesting is that in Revelation 4, we're told that the Almighty Holy One sits on the throne. So how can the Lamb stand in the middle of the throne, unless he stands at the very center of the One who sits on the throne? The profound implication here is that Jesus Christ—the Lion of the tribe of Judah, the Root of David, the little Lamb—comes from and stands in the very center of the being of the God who is almighty and holy.

This is why only Jesus—and no one else—is worthy to open the scroll. He stands at the very center of the being of God. Now feel the drama of this vision a little more. John says that the Lamb "took the scroll from the right hand of him who sat on the throne" (Revelation 5:7). The Lamb just walks up and takes the scroll out of the Almighty's hand. "And when he had taken it, the four living creatures and the twenty-four elders fell down before the Lamb" (Revelation 5:8). Of course they fell down. What else can you do before the Lamb? He stands at the very center of the being of God. That's why it's so utterly appropriate that the living creatures began to worship the Lamb, that the angelic hosts join in that worship, and that John hears the roar of acclamation from every created thing—in heaven, on earth, under the earth, in the sea—all crying out with joy to the Lamb. Mary's little Lamb is worthy of the same adoration as the Almighty God, because the Lamb who was slain comes from and stands out of the very center of the being of God. Wow! What a picture.

How does this vision clear our vision of earth? It does so in four ways.

THE LAMB KNOWS AND FEELS OUR SUFFERING

First, put on Revelation 5 glasses, and we realize that at the heart of reality is Someone who suffers. Isaiah put it best when speaking of the Lamb of God: "He was despised and rejected by men, a man of sorrows, and familiar with suffering" (Isaiah 53:3).

When you put on these glasses, you realize that we're never alone in our suffering. The Lamb is there at the center, and he still bears the marks of the worst suffering imaginable. We can echo the words of the spiritual: "Nobody knows the trouble I've seen / Nobody knows but Jesus." The Lamb does know; the throne feels human suffering. This is also why followers of the Lamb can never avoid suffering. The closer we get to the heart of the Lamb, the closer we get to a heart that bleeds for the suffering of the world.

THE LAMB IS FULL OF GRACE

Second, put on Revelation 5 glasses, and we realize that at the heart of reality stands One who is full of grace. Why did the Lion become a Lamb? Why did the Lamb suffer? Why was he slain? For the sake of the sheep. Again, Isaiah expresses it best: "We all, like sheep, have gone astray, each of us has turned to his own way; and the LORD has laid on [the Lamb of God] the iniquity of us all" (Isaiah 53:6).

The Lamb goes to the cross because of us; the Lamb goes to the cross for us; he goes to the Cross instead of us, to take upon himself the punishment that should justly go to us because of the sins of the world. There he stands—the sacrifice, the substitute, the satisfaction—in the very center of the throne. This picture cries out, "Come. Just come, just as you are." The heart of the Almighty, the heart of the Holy One, is the heart of the little Lamb who freely gave his life that we might be pardoned, and who freely receives any who come in repentance, and who freely pours out his sevenfold spirit on those who come. Grace, fullness of grace, is at that throne, and so the writer of the book of Hebrews calls it "the throne of grace" (Hebrews 4:16).

THE LAMB IS THE WAY TO FULLNESS OF LIFE

Third, put on Revelation 5 glasses, and we realize that the way of the Lamb is the way to the fullness of life. The way of servanthood, the way of sacrifice, the way of surrender is the way to the fullness of life. The Lion gets to the throne, but only by becoming a Lamb—a little Lamb—who gives his life for others. Now the Lamb isn't foolish; remember that he has seven eyes, which makes him immensely wise. And the Lamb isn't weak; he has seven horns, which means that he's immensely powerful. But here's the secret of this vision—a secret few people know, a secret we would never discover with our ordinary glasses: The greatest power in the universe is the weakness of sacrificial love. The greatest wisdom in the universe is the foolishness of sacrificial love.

The apostle Paul calls Christ crucified "the power of God and the wisdom of God" (1 Corinthians 1:24). The way of the Lamb is the wisest and most powerful way to live. What is the way of the Lamb? During his earthly life and ministry, the Lamb spoke:

Blessed are the poor in spirit, for theirs is the kingdom of heaven.

Blessed are those who mourn, for they will be comforted.

Blessed are the meek, for they will inherit the earth.

Blessed are those who hunger and thirst for righteousness, for they will be filled.

Blessed are the merciful, for they will be shown mercy.

Blessed are the pure in heart, for they will see God.

Blessed are the peacemakers, for they will be called sons of God.

Blessed are those who are persecuted because of righteousness, for theirs is the kingdom of heaven. . . .

You have heard that it was said, "Eye for eye, and tooth for tooth." But I tell you, Do not resist an evil person. If someone strikes you on the right cheek, turn to him the other also. And if someone wants to sue you and take your tunic, let him have your cloak as well. If someone forces you to go one mile, go with him two miles. Give to the one who asks you, and do not turn away from the one who wants to borrow from you (Matthew 5:3-10, 38-42).

Foolishness, weakness—if you are wearing ordinary glasses. Put on Revelation 5 glasses, and what seems weak is powerful, what seems foolish is wise. In fact, put on Revelation 5 glasses, and what the world calls wisdom turns out to be foolishness, and what the world calls power turns out to be utter weakness. Through Revelation 5 glasses you discover that the apostle Paul is right, that "God chose the foolish things of the world to shame the wise; God chose the weak things of the world to shame the strong" (1 Corinthians 1:27). Let the image grab you. The Lion does not win by being a lion. The Lion overcomes by becoming a Lamb, a little Lamb, a sacrificial Lamb. . . . Foolish? Weak? Not when you put on Revelation 5 glasses. There you discover the sacrificial life is the way to live fully human and fully alive.

Fourth, put on Revelation 5 glasses, and we realize where it's all going. It's all moving to the feet of the Lamb. When the Lamb breaks the seals of the scroll, we discover that everything—even the forces arranged against him—serves his purposes. That's the message of the rest of the book of Revelation. Everything serves Jesus Christ. The scroll unrolls, and it rolls toward his kingdom. That's why we can never lose when we go the way of the weak and powerless Lamb. Oh, it might appear through our ordinary glasses that we'll lose out. But we never really lose. In fact, even if we have to die going the way of the Lamb, we don't lose, because we know the secret. We know who is on the throne and who has the last word. It all ends at the feet of the resurrected and reigning Lamb. Only that which is consistent with his rule will endure. Only that which can be embraced by his rule will stand in the end.

So, if we want to grow, there must first be a change in our basic vision—a change in our basic presuppositions about life. Put on new glasses and leave them on. Look! A throne with Someone sitting on it, and in the very middle of the throne, the Lamb as if slain. And I hear all of creation joining in the burst of joy: "'To him who sits on the throne and to the Lamb be praise and honor and glory and power, for ever and ever!' The four living creatures said, 'Amen,' and the elders fell down and worshiped" (Revelation 5:13, 14).

Of course. What else do you do before such a Lamb?

© Darrell W. Johnson. Used with permission. This article was adapted from a sermon by Darrell W. Johnson, and originally published on Preaching Today Audio or PreachingToday.com, resources of Christianity Today International.

Look, a Great White Horse!

Christ's future victory gives us hope, strengthens our faith in him, and reinforces our endurance.

by R. Geoffrey Brown

We can't seem to comprehend some things in the book of Revelation. But other things are clear, and we can understand them easily. When we read of the fall of Babylon; when we see the overthrow of the false prophet, the beast, and the dragon; when we behold the great white horse and a rider with his vesture dipped in blood, and upon the thigh of that rider is written the name "KING OF KINGS AND LORD OF LORDS" (Revelation 19:16) . . . When we see all of this, there can be no doubt. What we are seeing can be understood. It is nothing less than the great triumph and victory of Jesus Christ the Lord, a victory that we'll participate in!

Think of what John's vision in Revelation 19 means. Once Jesus was despised and rejected of men, yet in the coming hour every knee shall bow—ours too. Once men railed on him with their tongues, yet in that hour every tongue will confess that Jesus Christ is Lord—ours too. Once he responded with silence, yet in that hour his voice will rock and shake Heaven and earth—we will hear it. Once they put a crimson robe on his back and mocked him, yet in that hour he will wear the crimson vestures of his triumphant atonement—and we shall see him. Once twelve humble men followed him about, yet on that day the whole company of angels will follow in his train—we will be with them. Once they pressed a crown of thorns upon his head and brow, yet in his glory he will wear many crowns upon his head—and we will be there.

Revelation 19 declares that all wrongs will be right. This rider on his great white horse, crowned with many crowns, will come to shake the golden chain of justice for us. The thundering hoofbeats will say, "All is right. It's all right at last."

I'd like to take you, if I could, to a graphic portrayal of the Word of God in a great cathedral in Milan. Come in out of the glare of the Italian sunshine, pass through the cathedral doors, and suddenly see stretching out before you one of Europe's largest cathedrals, where fifty-two marbled columns hold up the lofty, octagonal dome, with over 4,400 turrets and pinnacles. Statues of angels rise all about us, and the effect is one of an incomparable combination of grace and grandeur, beauty and vastness.

Up front behind the altar, like a window opening out of Heaven, is one of the largest stained glass windows in the world. Depicted here is not an Old Testament scene. That stained glass window does not depict the resurrection of Jesus Christ the Lord, not his crucifixion or ascension. With tremendous imagery that window depicts the triumph of Jesus Christ the Lord. The afternoon sun strains in, turning the window into a sea of glass mingled with fire. You see the vials being outpoured, the trumpets, Michael and his angels in battle against the dragon; you see the great angel with the rainbow upon his head, one foot upon the earth and the other upon the heavens, declaring in the name of him who lives forever and ever that time shall be no longer. Bound with a chain, Satan is thrown into the bottomless pit at last. The great white throne glows in the sunlight. Most impressive of all is the great white horse. Upon the horse sits a still greater rider with the armies of Heaven behind him. He comes to set everything straight at last for every one of us who has hoped in him, and for everyone who has been subjected to the pain and prejudice of living for Jesus Christ in a world seemingly gone mad.

Why do I want to take you into this cathedral at Milan? Because we can sit together and contemplate this wondrous triumph of Jesus Christ the Lord at the end. It is there we may understand the necessity of an invincible faith in this triumph. And it's there we may understand that this triumph comes for Christ, by Christ, and through Jesus Christ alone. Listen to the words of the old spiritual: "Nobody knows the trouble I've seen / Nobody knows but Jesus / Nobody knows the trouble I've seen / Glory Hallelujah." The "Glory Hallelujah" is put at the end because Jesus is going to return for a final triumph over the trouble I've seen. Nothing can stop him. That makes an indelible statement on the sufferings of this present life.

We read assurance of the victory of our cause in Revelation 19:11-13: "I saw heaven standing open and there before me was a white horse, whose rider is called Faithful and True. With justice he judges and makes war. His eyes are like blazing fire, and on his head are many crowns. He has a name written on him that no one knows but he himself. He is dressed in a robe dipped in blood, and his name is the Word of God."

CHRIST'S FUTURE VICTORY GIVES US HOPE

This vision of victory is necessary for our hope, faith, and endurance. Because we live in an age where we see far too much, we see far too little. But what we do see sometimes seems so strong that it makes our faith seem weak. So, in a sense, we must have this vitamin supplement of the book of Revelation, where we clearly see the triumph of the truth and the principles that are spoken of throughout the Bible. In Revelation, we see the arc that spans the stormy history of the ages. We listen to thunder rolls on the last great day when the kingdoms of this world become the kingdom of our Lord and his Christ. Resplendent with glory, it makes the brightest day in human history look like midnight. It makes our sufferings—I don't want to make light of them—pale in significance before the triumph and the glories to be revealed.

If this vision was necessary for the early church, when the pagan Roman Empire was trying to drown the church in its own blood, then how much more is it still necessary to us in this day when the Antichrist puts on this mask, that mask, and tries to fool us with delusions and tries to call us with perversion.

Don't you get weary of the evil of our day? In the book of Revelation, John sees the vision of the wicked beast that received a deathblow. As the wound spouts blood, the beast goes away to hide for a while. Then that beast comes forward again with its deathblow healed, and all of the earth follows after to worship it. In a sense that's what we see today: evil in men and women, evil in institutions, evil in ourselves. We give it the death stroke; it goes away; it comes back strong.

We ask, "Why?" It can be discouraging. We comfort ourselves with the truth that God can bring good out of evil, but we still say, "Why evil at all? Why doesn't God destroy evil?" The great answer that the Bible gives in Revelation 19:11 is, *Look! A great white horse with a still greater rider.* And the answer is the certainty, the indisputable happening in the future of the triumph over evil.

When Robinson Crusoe's good man Friday asked him, "Why doesn't God destroy the devil?" Robinson Crusoe gave him the right answer, the only answer, the great answer. He said, "God will destroy him."

That's the comfort for us. We see the ebb and flow of history. We see the aspirations of human beings who want to reach high, yet grovel low in the bloody panorama of history. We see the church in ceaseless battle with the devil. That's not all we see. Look there on that stained glass window in the cathedral of Milan, a great white horse. Here we see the end of evil. We see the Lamb of God standing on Mount Zion. We see all things put under his feet. We see him riding the great white horse, and with him are all the armies of Heaven coming in his train. We see this world of strife and wickedness and sin and bitterness and hatred and blood and death. We see this whole world suddenly locked into the glory of God, and the new heavens and the new earth, wherein dwells righteousness—not in some temporal passing fashion as a fugitive visitor, but as the eternal unbroken order for all eternity. We gain the strength to go on, to face tomorrow, because we know what's going to happen at last.

CHRIST'S FUTURE VICTORY STRENGTHENS OUR FAITH IN HIM

The triumph of the victory and righteousness of Jesus Christ will come for him, by him, and through him alone. Some will tell you that triumph will come by the development of human beings—the gradual evolution of their potentialities. We should just give it time, wait and see. Everything's coming up roses. But can we really trust human progress to stop people and nations from sinning? Will human progress and achievement ever wipe away all tears from our eyes or heal our broken hearts? To ask these questions is to answer them. "No." The final victory will not come through some natural progress of human development or through the religious forces operating in the world right now. The victory will come not by an improvement of the present order, but through its complete overthrow and supersession.

The high point of human history will be the sudden appearance on the field of battle of the captain of our salvation. And he will come in glory, and it will be comparable to what John beheld: *Look, I see a great white horse. And there is a rider on that horse whose name is Faithful and True, and there are many crowns upon his head.* That's what we see in the cathedral of Milan when we look at the splendor of that stained glass window, one of the largest in the world. What do we come away with when we leave the cathedral of Milan and when we feel like no one understands our suffering? We realize that Christ's victory means the end of all those who oppress us, of all those who've ever mocked us or put us down or tried to confound the progress of the kingdom of God.

When the army of Julian the Apostate was on the march to Persia, some of the soldiers got hold of a Christian believer to torment and torture him in brutal sport. After they wearied of it, they looked into his eyes and said to their helpless victim, with infinite scorn in their voices, "And your Jesus—what is your carpenter of Nazareth doing now?" The prisoner looked up through pain, blood, and agony to say, "He is building a coffin for your emperor."

It's true! For every God-defying person, every God-defying power, and every God-defying principle that exalts itself against God and his Word, the coffin is now being built. You can be assured that when Christ comes to conquer, he will call you into his train, and he will pronounce the divine doom upon all wicked civilizations and inhuman forms of cruelty and lust. Doomed are all the enemies of God, totally and universally, throughout the entire earth.

CHRIST'S FUTURE VICTORY REINFORCES OUR ENDURANCE

In Ashtabula, Ohio, in 1876, a train went off the tracks and over the bridge, and many people were killed. One of those who died was Reverend P. P. Bliss, a hymn writer and great evangelist. One of his most famous hymns was "Hold the Fort." It was written after the Civil War, marking the occasion when Atlanta had been besieged and General Hood, for the Southern armies, came up and tried to draw away Sherman's army. Hood wasn't successful, but he did have a couple of victories. One of them was at Alatoona Pass, where he attacked. At that point Sherman was on Kennesaw Mountain, a distance away. He looked down and could see that his beleaguered troops were losing it, and so Sherman heliographed to them, "Hold the fort, I am coming."

Major Whittle, a member of Sherman's army, later recounted the tale to Bliss, who used it as the inspiration for his famous hymn: "'Hold the fort, for I am coming!' / Jesus signals still / Wave the answer back to Heaven / 'By Thy grace, we will!'"

The message from the rider on the great white horse to you, his church, is, *Occupy until I come. Hold the fort, for I am coming.* Jesus might come at the midnight watch. He might come at the third watch. He might come at the fourth watch, as he did on the Sea of Galilee to his frightened disciples caught in the storm. Whatever time he arrives, "It will be good for those servants whose master finds them watching when he comes. I tell you the truth, he will dress himself to serve, will have them recline at the table and will come and wait on them" (Luke 12:37). That's what day is coming. What a glorious day it will be. Then you will not be the least bit sorry you kept the faith and fought the battle and finished the course that God had given you.

That's why the Word of God tells us to live now with this great hope in our hearts. We leave this great cathedral of Milan and go out into the Italian sunshine, and we go out with the shine of the Son of God in our hearts. Lift high your hearts. Lift them up! Our king will come. Our cause will conquer. When the world's sky is darkest with the clouds of unbelief, behold the glory of the coming of the Lord. He is trampling out the vintage where the grapes of wrath are stored. Behold, he's coming! And above all the chariots and above all the horsemen comes the rider on the great white horse. When the babble sounds are loudest in their scornful derision of the church of God and his eternal Son, and you as a believer in Jesus Christ are derided for that, you shall hear, floating down from Heaven, the notes of that distant triumph song, whose sweet melody shall one day encompass the heavens and the earth like the wonderful words of the "Hallelujah" chorus from Handel's *Messiah*: "Hallelujah, hallelujah! For the Lord God Omnipotent reigneth. The kingdom of this world is become the Kingdom of our Lord, and of His Christ, and he shall reign forever and ever!"

Yes, he shall. And yes, truly, nobody knows the sorrows and trouble I've seen. Nobody knows my sorrows. But most true of all is another spiritual I haven't yet mentioned. Here's how it goes: "King Jesus rides on a milk-white horse / No man can a-hinder me / The river of Jordan he did cross / No man can a-hinder me / Ride on, King Jesus / No man can a-hinder me / Ride on, King Jesus / No man can a-hinder me."

FIND SPIRITUAL FORMATION TOOLS at Christian BibleStudies.com

- ▶ Join over **125,000 people** who use ChristianBibleStudies.com

- ▶ Choose from **over 800 downloadable Bible studies** to find exactly what you're looking for

- ▶ Study through a book of the Bible **verse-by-verse**, discuss an important topic from Scripture, or learn about **hot topics** like movies and politics

- ▶ Pay only once and make up to **1,000 copies**

- ▶ Enhance your personal devotions, small groups, or Sunday School classes

- ▶ Facilitate **lively discussions** with fascinating topics

a service of

CHRISTIANITY TODAY
INTERNATIONAL

BUILD AN EFFECTIVE MINISTRY with Small Groups.com

Inspiring
Life-Changing
Community

- Learn how to **start or re-start** both small groups and entire ministries

- Choose from thousands of **training tools, Bible studies, and free articles** from trusted leaders like Philip Yancey, Les and Leslie Parrott, and Larry Crabb

- Connect your group with a free and fun **social-networking tool**

- **Train yourself and your leaders** with invaluable assessments and orientation guides

- Downloadable resources are ready for **immediate use** and can be copied up to 1,000 times

- Join the **blog conversation** and share your small-group experiences

a service of

CHRISTIANITY TODAY
INTERNATIONAL